Ruby Mountain

poems by

Ruth Nolan

Finishing Line Press
Georgetown, Kentucky

Ruby Mountain

*For my beloved daughter Tarah
and her beautiful baby boys, Simon and Luke*

Copyright © 2016 by Ruth Nolan
ISBN 978-1-63534-054-9 First Edition
All rights reserved under International and Pan-American Copyright Conventions. No part of this book may be reproduced in any manner whatsoever without written permission from the publisher, except in the case of brief quotations embodied in critical articles and reviews.

ACKNOWLEDGMENTS

Many people have contributed their support, friendship, and feedback towards my completion of this manuscript. I'd like to acknowledge and thank Philip Helland, Juan Felipe Herrera, Gayle Brandeis, Tim Z. Hernandez, Stephanie Barbe Hammer, Jill Alexander Essbaum, Michelle Meyering Franke, Chad Sweeney, Anthony McCann, Gayle Wattawa, Malcolm Margolin, Antonia Crane, Lisa Henry, Brandi Spaethe, Natashia Deon, Robert Romanus, Marion Mitchell-Wilson, Mike Sleboda, my wonderful writing students and colleagues at College of the Desert, my beloved Inlandia Institute Writing Workshop members, and my extended family. There are so many others whose names are too numerous to include here, but I thank all of you, too! I'd also like to acknowledge the real-life Willie Boy and Carlota Mike, without whose tragic-beautiful Mojave Desert story this book would not have been inspired. I offer you both - as well as your descendants who live in the California deserts today - honor and respect for what you endured for love in 1909

Publisher: Leah Maines

Editor: Christen Kincaid

Cover Art: Ruth Nolan

Author Photo: Pablo Aguilar

Cover Design: Elizabeth Maines

Printed in the USA on acid-free paper.
Order online: www.finishinglinepress.com
also available on amazon.com

Author inquiries and mail orders:
Finishing Line Press
P. O. Box 1626
Georgetown, Kentucky 40324
U. S. A.

Table of Contents

Anniversary Five 1
Beautiful Remains 2
Berkeley Marina 4
Black-chinned Hummingbird 6
Blythe Intaglios 7
Carlota 8
Crucifixion 9
Death Valley Junction 10
Deep Canyon 12
The Fix 13
Foreclosure / Word Spit 14
Ghost Dance / Wovoka 15
Hundred Year Flood 16
Last Manhunt 17
Late November Pantoum 18
Nodding Off 20
Mr. and Mrs. End of the World 22
Panorama Fire 23
Pool Guy 24
Ruby Mountain 25
Searchlight 27
Tank Man 29
Thirteen Tuesdays of St. Anthony 30
U-Haul Villanelle 31
The Ying Yang and the Cross 32
Tortoise Heaven 34
What Rises 35

"If the doors of perception were cleansed,
everything would appear to man as it truly is: infinite"
—from "The Marriage of Heaven and Hell," William Blake

"Love is hard"
—from *the Hunt for Willie Boy: Indian Hating & Popular Culture*
James A. Sandos & Larry E. Burgess

Anniversary Five
2015

Shouldn't I visit your grave
shouldn't I buy flowers for you
shouldn't I hug your friends
shouldn't I imagine you, hard
shouldn't I call your mother
shouldn't I tell you off
shouldn't I tell you I love you
shouldn't I burn your journal
shouldn't I wear your watch
shouldn't I release a balloon
shouldn't I swim laps to the moon
shouldn't I write a memoir
shouldn't I flirt with hummingbirds
shouldn't I wash your sheets
shouldn't I touch your shirt
shouldn't I yell at you, then cry
shouldn't I slap you in the face
shouldn't I push your car off a cliff
shouldn't I hike in your memory
shouldn't I look for your passport
shouldn't I pretend you did it for love
shouldn't I believe it was a mistake
shouldn't I wonder why not
shouldn't I wonder why
shouldn't you have done it somewhere ugly
shouldn't you have spared the pretty hills

Suicide is the 10th leading cause of death in the U.S.
—The Centers for Disease Control, 2015

Beautiful Remains
Yuha Desert, California

I saw three golden eagles
on the morning of the night
of an all-night mourning ceremony
sponsored by Kumeyaay Indians
who for centuries have called
this part of the desert home.

I saw three golden eagles on the night of
a night-long mourning ceremony
for the eagles being killed
for the tortoises being killed
for the tall Ocotillo being killed
for all that is being sacrificed
in the name of renewable energy.

The first eagle landed
in the fast lane
of I-60 in the Badlands
and was waiting there.
He lifted slowly
as I approached
on my way along the lonely
drive to the ceremony.

The second eagle
was painted on a truck
on I-10 near Palm Springs
and rode beside me
for more than 30 miles
the Santa Ana winds
at our backs, taller
than life or wind towers.

The third eagle
was a fine piece of art
carved into the bolero tie
of the tribal chairman
in ivory white, every
fine detail of feather
chiseled like wind hearts.

I'm telling you this story
because it's true
because all three eagles
flew above our heads
while the men shook rattles
and sang bird songs
all night long from sunset
to dawn, because we all wept
on the hill by the medicine wheel
and then the sun grew too warm
and the wind refused to howl.

Berkeley Marina
Western Wilderness Conference, Cal Berkeley, April 9, 2010

Doing the calculations
over and over again in my head
while driving through the breasted Badlands
while tonguing the hole of my missing tooth
while stroking the impossibly soft kitty
while trying to go to sleep alone at 3:00 AM
over and over again in my head
doing the calculations.

When going over it in my head
again and again, I calculate

that it happened right as I bit into
the warm chocolate chip cookie
handed to me by the desk clerk
at the Berkeley Marina Hotel.

I calculate
as I go over it again and again
that it may have happened as I was
resting my head on the soft down pillow
it's kind of like guessing
the moment of my daughter's conception
I can come close
but I'll never know for sure
and the moment of your death
is much more of a pressing issue
it's a birth that never arrives
just the aftershock, again and again.

When I go over and over it again and again
in my head, as I do at 3:00 AM trying to sleep
by myself, without you
I pretend for just a moment
that the kitty is the reincarnation of you
the eyes, so much like yours
the aloof attitude
but the always-returning
your eyes, like hers.

I calculate, as I drive through the Badlands
80 mph with my wheels barely clinging
to the edge of death drop curves
even in the fog, or because of the fog.

I calculate, and measure, and weigh the
memory of what I was doing at just that
exact second—when I stood at the edge
of the Martin Luther King Jr. Student Center
Balcony at Cal Berkeley and saw the
Golden Gate Bridge suddenly loom into
vision through the fog—or maybe

it was when I bought you a tie-dye shirt
from a street vendor, knowing how much you
loved to wear clothes with colors that swirled
together like let-free human blood.

I calculate that it was the moment
that I bit into the warm chocolate chip cookie
and saw the bridge through the fog and
remembered the last time we had sex and
how much I loved your eyes when they
sometimes went from green to blue
and the lecture I was supposed to give
and the gift from the desk clerk that was
a warrant for your impending death.

I think it happened right then.
That was when you put the barrel end
of the shotgun in your mouth
then bit down hard, the way you
used to clamp onto my
nipples and tongue
then kissed the world goodbye
still hanging on to me.

Black-chinned Hummingbird
A small hummingbird of The West

I cut fresh sage at the mouth of Wildrose Canyon
brought it home to dry on the old wood stove.
I want to burn the fat string-wrapped bundles
so I can remember you, so I can forget about you.

The kitchen table is full of stems and memories
of hikes in the Panamints, but your knife is dull.
I've been hiking old and new desert trails alone
the hills, the dunes, the wind, pending solar farms.

I had to go so far to find this year's crop of sage.
Drought. The sky, blinded by technology's stare.
You once tried to mend the broken furniture
but wouldn't hug our daughter or braid her hair.

Outside, the black-chinned hummingbird builds
its little nest in blades of a lone, far-north palm tree,
weaving together dried grass and other lost things,
threads of your flannel shirt that I still love to wear.

I wonder how long it will survive in the next hot
windstorm in this season without rain, a summer full
of huge mirrors and blades, if the fat turkey vultures
will pluck its young from broken shells, then fly away.

Blythe Intaglios

Barrio Cuchillo
Gabriel the white goose
fights six small dogs

Almost spring
ghost flower
to the south

Silver lip gloss moon
Big Maria Mountains
time to fall in love

Smoking meth
season of melting ice

Bouse Fisherman
carved on desert pavement
the spear points north

Two Chihuahuas jump the fence

Carlota

Centuries after the whole world was frozen
secretaries find two letters
in the archives of the Indian boarding school

The letters concern a 16-year-old Chemehuevi girl
taken forcibly from her home
at the Oasis of Mara, also known as 29 Palms
along with other Indian children
from across the southwestern U.S.

> *April 21, 1909*
> Dear Mr. and Mrs. Augustine, your daughter Carlota
> will be returning home. She screams and cries all the time,
> says she sees demons and witches near the outhouse.
> We believe she has a secret lover, an Indian boy
> she wants to run away with, but this is not good for her.
> She is frightening the other children. She must go home.
>
> *April 22, 1909*
> Dear Mr. and Mrs. Augustine, your daughter Carlota
> passed away this morning. She woke up and was fine,
> and later, she lay down to take a nap and was found dead.

The wagon carrying the body of Carlota
caught up to the horse of the rider
who was taking the first letter
to Mr. and Mrs. Augustine.
The horse was tied to a pinyon tree
and its rider was missing. Spooked,
the driver of the wagon carrying Carlota's body
turned around. She was buried at a cemetery
beneath what's now the 215 freeway in Menifee.

This is Carlota's story
sung in the key of sand dunes
the harmonies of vanishing suns

Crucifixion

The Easter eggs are gone
the kitty stalks a chicken
late winter rains bless us
even though it's spring
good thing the flowers
point to their own undoing
at a sun that loves them
too much, they sacrifice
water to the full mirage,
decades of empty canyons
for an hour of flash flood,
cat's claw and empty shells.

Death Valley Junction

The way he told the story
that night I stopped by the Amargosa Hotel
where dancer Marta Beckett
painted the walls of the old Opera House
with pictures of people
so she wouldn't have to dance
to an empty room
while wild horses and dust devils
raced across the scorched desert floor nearby
that long story, told by the old man at the front desk,
it was first about the Tonopah Tidewater Railroad
and then about the museum right there
in Death Valley Junction
filed with tiny trains, tracks, a perfect facsimile
of the old railroad itself,
even the re-creation of a ghost town called Evelyn
on the road to Shoshone close to
eagle Mountain, that lonely hunk by the road,
an old railroad stop of a town, Evelyn,
all gone now except for one tall pine tree
standing all by itself and still alive
and then he offered me free coffee, the last of the pot
it was 5:32 PM in early January
halfway between Furnace Creek and Shoshone
a moonless night, pitch dark already
and he was an old man
and he told me a story about an old place
in Apple Valley, at the edge of the Mojave, where I grew up
a place over-run with Walmarts, suburbia, freeways
not the Joshua Tree forests I once wandered through
and it was a story about the Red Barn ruins
at the corner of Central Road and Highway 18
he said he had owned the Red Barn in 1962
and it was burned down
by a jealous lover—an unknown Hollywood starlet—
who was angry at her lover, a small time cowboy movie star
who was best friends with Roy Rogers
who founded the town of Apple Valley in 1947
and Roy himself once eyed me like cool water
at the Apple Valley Country Club when I was 17
and the old man here in Death Valley Junction
on this black night spoke of fire
of a ruins I knew so well
the one I'd drive by in my youth so many times

never knowing what it was, not that I cared
and the ghost of Marta Becket fills this room
her voice, her photos, the faint smell of propane
and the last thing I heard
as I edged towards the heavy door to the place
to go back into that heartless night
and drive back to my small cabin by myself
hoping I wouldn't break down
since I was far beyond cell phone range
was to look for the tree
when I drove past the old town of Evelyn
thousands of miles away from my ancestral homes:
Ireland, so green and tragic
that my father cut it off like a broken thumb,
the land of the Iroquois, my maternal home
filtering down through my indigenous genes,
and homeless, I keep wandering here
and on that deeply unmoored drive
I saw it, I swear, I saw the tree, in the dark
(without looking away from the road)
nestled in the shoulder of Eagle Mountain
and pointing the way to a faceful of stars
the rush of wind in my face
I didn't look, but I saw it
and I just know it's still there, tucked in
by Orion's Belt, sipping from the Big Dipper
while I dream of perfect desert symphonies
operas and dancers and high season trains
full of well-dressed visitors, lovers, and gems
of a tree name Evelyn, soothing every traveler
who drives by here looking
for the Wild West, looking for railroad tracks
and old songs and for all things that have been lost
and lived and rooted down somehow
in the Mojave's deep, unbroken soul.

> *Evelyn is a ghost town that once serviced the Tonopah Tidewater Railroad as a stop between Death Valley Junction and Shoshone, California, along what is now State Highway 127. Although all of the old buildings have burned down, including the tiny schoolhouse, parts of the old railroad remain, and the site of Evelyn is marked by a single remaining pine tree that has survived.*

Deep Canyon

I.
Sunrise
two VIP tickets
        to Coachella Fest
sit on my desk

you left
        a song
        without sound

the music festival goes on
without us

II.
Two dragonflies

the blue one

        loses a wing

April is endless sky

The Fix
> *I just died in your arms tonight*

You say it's your birthday
someday, we'll be together

I've been through the desert on a horse with no name
welcome to the Hotel California

love hurts, love scars, love wounds, and mars
one thing leads to another

girlfriend in a coma, I know, I know it's really serious
well, she's walking through the clouds with a circus mind

break on through to the other side
this bird has flown

take anything you want from me
fly on, little wing.

Foreclosure / Word Spit

I should buy a house in Palm Springs
I should cook bacon and eggs
I should get out of this blue bathrobe
I should get out of my Casper bed
I should perform a candle ceremony
I should rip out cemetery grass
I should grade compare/contrast essays
I should hike to Deep Creek Hot Springs
I should lift a leg, text my pregnant daughter
I should go to the gynecologist
I should get high with younger men
I should look out across city lights with them
I should not apologize for my cough
I should probably be married
I should give courtesy hand jobs
I should think about short sales
I should clean the pool by myself
I should dream about grandchildren
I should be homeless, living on roofs
I should be starting over again.

Ghost Dance / Wovoka
from the New Messiah, 1909

I am spirit
    You must make a dance to continue five days.

I am wind
    My heart is full of gladness for the gifts you have brought me.

I am mountain
    When you get home I shall give you good cloud.

I am rain
    I give you a good spirit and give you all good paint.

I am sky
    You must not fight. Do right always.

I am lake
    Do not tell the white people about this.

I am star
    The dead are still alive again.

I am awake
    Do not refuse to work for the whites, and do not make any trouble.

I am unborn
    When the earth shakes at the coming of the new world, do not be afraid. You will receive good words again from me.

I survive
    The water will return. The people will be whole again.

Dance until my return.

There will be love.

Hundred Year Flood

At the end of ZZYZX Road
where the Mojave River ends
this place, once a health resort
built by drug addicts and felons
imported from Skid Row in L.A.
named so it would be the last word
in the English language dictionary
by a health-food-preaching, 8th-grade dropout
who had two P.O. Boxes in Baker
    one for his food-supplement business
    one for his Dr. Curtis Springer commentaries
    aired through the Mojave by radio
you can go to deep end of the desert, and find tranquility
where the floodwaters have left their pressures behind:
cottonwood, twisted cars, suburban garbage
delivered insanely northward and left behind
at the bottom of this inland sea which looks deep
but is almost always powder dry
with the face of an angel
like Borax cleanser in tin cans.

Sometimes, flash floods
overflow the dam at the Forks of the Mojave River
and course down into the desert like a vintage roller coaster
on creaking tracks. Manifest Destiny came through here
too, following the ancient river flood plain
carrying old bits of wagon boards from Mormon settlers
who followed a page of Catholic Bible torn from Father Garces
who led the minions out of this forsaken zone
who frowned at the rough men of the Wild West
    who slaughtered stray Chemuehuevi or Shoshone
    who fished the Mojave Tui Chub into extinction
    who opened the flood gates
    for a desert river
    that doesn't behave
    like a river should.

Last Manhunt

He is one of us
living on both sides of the fence
living on his second breath and
singing Wovoka's Ghost Dance
singing of palm tree revivals
singing of lizards sipping at faint oases
of a mid-day sun tearing flesh from breasts
of an early-morning hangman's noose
of the visions of an in-between world
running through Joshua tree forests
running past the shotgun marks on rocks
running beyond where night finds day
wearing his ghost shirt
immune to bullets
immune to railroads
immune to the absence of rain
immune to gold
and when we come
to remember him
to remember his shadow
the tracks he left behind
where it's rumored
that he found his death
his memory will speak to us
and we will remember
that he will have remembered
> *I have inhabited this town*
> *and I have passed you by*
> *and I am blind to it again*
> *and I have remembered*
> *and I will show you again*
> *that this is how*
> *the arrow flies*

Late November Pantoum

I thought our love was a thunderstorm, rain hitting the rake
naked by the pool, sunrise, July, unafraid of lightning
I was devoted to me and you were devoted to you, I loved
the kitty coffee mug I borrowed from your mother's house.

Naked by the pool, sunrise, July, unafraid of lightning
in the Mojave in May, the cup's handle snapped in September
the kitty coffee mug I borrowed from your mother's house
I'm walking to my morning poetry class, students waiting.

In the Mojave in May, the cup's handle snapped in September
reading the Beat poets today, the boil of Ginsberg's "Howl"
I'm walking to my morning poetry class, students waiting
I've overheated the cup today, November, I burn my hand.

Reading the Beat poets today, the boil of Ginsberg's "Howl"
love at the Box Springs Mountains, your hands on my breasts
I've overheated the cup today, November, I burn my hand
parked in my car, leaning over to me, your fingers are cold.

Love at the Box Springs Mountains, your hands on my breasts
coyotes in the boulders, nipping berries from Juniper trees
parked in my car, leaning over to me, your fingers are cold
the desert, my poetry students, my dogs, I wonder where I am.

Coyotes in the boulders, nipping berries from Juniper trees
we held each other and the hot rain ran down across our toes
the desert, my poetry students, my dogs, I wonder where I am
"America" is another poem we'll study today, where are you?

We held each other, and the hot rain ran down across our toes
summer in the desert compressed us into one frozen bone
"America" is another poem we'll study today, where are you?
I'm obliged to teach my students how to explicate a poem.

Summer in the desert compressed us into one frozen bone
you initiate sex with me, then go off to sleep all alone
I'm obliged to teach my students how to explicate a poem
and the animals are satiated now, nosing into winter holes.

You initiate sex with me, then go off to sleep all alone
I brew a fresh pot of coffee, the dog's scars are nearly gone
and the animals are satiated now, nosing towards winter holes
I loved you because you pulled me into a violent thunderstorm.

I brew a fresh pot of coffee, my dog's scars are nearly gone
you wrapped me in your arms and your heart was beating warm
I loved you because you pulled me into a violent thunderstorm
broken cup, silent desert, I rake my voice across another poem.

Nodding Off

Here,
The pretty hills
The pretty hills
Morning, 11 AM.

I see people circling on freeways
the circling
of red-tailed hawks above
ancestral Cahuilla land
in Redlands, Box Springs Mountains,
at the Santa Ana River
close to downtown Riverside
with its Mission Inn
realize there were no Mission Indians
only slaves
now the old Catholic mission on Barton Road
sits by Loma Linda hospital behavioral center
and the monument of de Anza
adjacent to the river
stippled with graffiti, urine, blood.

So I begin to live in circles
repeating the same affirmations
listening to NASA voyager recordings
of outer space over and over again
making the rounds from Palm Desert
past Chino Canyon, where all of
creation was begun
through the shouldered gap
of San Gorgonio Pass
through Badlands, Riverside, Redlands
the I-10 to the 60 to the 91 south
and looping back
passing Mary Jane Cemetery

and back home
after easing downhill
through the wind farms
I see open space
where once there was a tree, views
of the little San Bernardino Mountains
a bit more breeze
and I want to photograph the absence
frame it with memory, now I can see
familiar patterns of stars
a better view of passing satellites

tracing their faithful circumference
around the earth faster than planets do.

The pretty hills
The pretty hills
Morning, 11 AM.

The pretty hills

It will give me hope, I hope
I hope I hope I hope
that things really are connected
better this than the whip of thorny
cacti stinging me in the face
every time I stepped into the front yard
the sad fact of a bird's nest tossed
onto the ground by a blast of wind
the hooks of religions that rope us in
the dams that block us all
the demon intaglios can't be pulled
to the sea on the Colorado River
anymore from the tops of canyon walls
the water is re-assigned
before it reaches the sea

tell me there is no obsessive
compulsive desert here
just a smooth meditation
of people walking the same
pilgrimages, embellishing here
pruning here, entirely colonizing
over there, new volunteers
a deeper groove in the old flood
channels each time the heavy
rains push water over the top
magical strata revealed in rock
unimagined layers of sand
richer in color and theme
the same stories played out over
and over again, circularly

Red-tailed hawks
The pretty hills
The pretty hills

Morning, 11 AM
Ecstasy
LSD

Mr. and Mrs. End of the World

> *"I'm going to tell you these stories....but first, I'm going to break your heart."* Larry Eddy, Chemehuevi Salt Song Singer, 2009

It's the driest place in the world / come get wet with me over here

the agony of drought / the swagger of flash flood

day after day, no grass / all night long, every night

I hold clouds in my heart / let's get down with lawnmowers

my guitar is lonely in its case / I'm a music man, come into my arms

the sheer force of water / I'll love you with my favorite songs

my car begins to move / ain't no lack of love 'round here

the faces of my children rush by / come get wet with me

I know this is my time / see? the clouds are opening

time for rain, the dry wash / it's destiny, I will heal you

I am empty no more / look how white the sky is

the swagger of flash flood / the agony of drought

Panorama Fire

If I could sweep these smoke rings from my thighs
I might surmise a glare, a bite of lip
your smile would imitate the pink sunrise
eyes of ochre, a painter's fingertips
perhaps a fire would be stopped red-flare
a short-lived pause of light at mountain's head
snuff out this night, forget you do not care
but flames invite, they curl me to your side
you pause to glisten, ignorant of homes
coiled rattlesnakes that will be casualties
I hide behind embers, quiet-eyed as stones
I can't escape this fire, I will not try
the hills will burn tonight, I'll spring with love
you'll light a cigarette, the blue-flamed stove.

> *The Panorama Fire, located in the foothills of the San Bernardino Mountains, burned 280 homes to the ground and killed five people. It's considered one of the top 10 worst wildfires in California history.*

Pool Guy

If you could call me one more time
I'd say I'm looking at a raven sky

that the California desert isn't Israel
though our constellations are the same

I'd say that I'm overjoyed by pink
wildflower clouds in the garden, it's

April, and the tiny green oranges
you fingered grow bigger on the trees

I'd say that the dog I love is still
healing from his back injury

that I made a bit of extra cash from
selling the didgeridoo and shotgun

that the needled Palo Verde trees
are sprayed with yellow flowers

that the red-throated Costa's hummingbirds
suckle white sugar syrup from my feeder

that the sunflower seeds you scattered
with one toss of the hand are now sprouting

that the crows are occupying the tallest
palm though you once beat them away

I stare at algae blooming in the pool, pretend
I'm not waiting for you to add chlorine

that you didn't forsake me in the promised
land, this is not what I hired you to do.

Ruby Mountain
> *This is a real place*

Here: a grinding stone
there: a spray of bullet casings from 1909

Within: a barricaded hilltop where the ancestors
left red handprints, offered scorched bighorn skulls

Where: the lump rock backside
of the San Bernardino Mountains, elevation 3,722 feet

When: the granite blushes ruby red, sundown

Who: some would say you are an outlaw
Chemehuevi, Willie Boy, the Manhunt is on

What: you wanted the one you loved
ate lizards for her and puked them up

September and October
in the Mojave, too hot for words, too hot for her

Why: the posse thought she was you
beautiful Carlota, your cousin, in your overcoat

How: you barricaded yourself in the rocks
and the schoolteacher named Clara True
had to rescue the men you shot
but did not kill

Although: you tried to hide at 29 Palms
but your grandmother
threw your gun in the pond
Spirit Runner
your people have no word for suicide
you followed the old trail
to the other side
over there: shattered canyon
where the lovers
flew, so much and nothing
left behind, just everything

the sun, the stars
wheeling across the sky
forever the shape
and shift and shade
of fiery sunrise
of broken hearts

they say now that you never died
that you slipped away under cover of dark
leaving only bullet holes
sprayed across the Wonderland of Rocks.

Searchlight

It's another over-the-rainbow weekend.
I set sail and drive an eight hour arc
through California, Arizona Nevada
invited to participate in a protest
with an ex-lover who's a friend again
with the ex-lover's family, who hate my guts
with assorted acquaintances old and new
with three truckloads of Lake Havasu Indians.

I'm helping put a stop to the windmills
about to be built near Lake Mojave
wanting to see new life this spring
not life-giving land destroyed
before the flowers come along.

Hard to believe
there's a town called Searchlight
in the middle of the desert
hard to believe that nearby
there's a lake big enough for whitecaps
and boats going down
in summer squalls
that rise from nowhere
but it's late winter, the air is still.

We might be on and off again
(he asks for $80 for white medicine, says
we'll make love again, but not right now)
my instincts know the way home
(so I don't have to think or feel too much)
through ancient Joshua Tree forests
past the ugly solar towers at Stateline
for solid ground, the desert once

was almost entirely under water
and sometimes on these long
solitary drives I feel like I'm sailing
the desert so often feels like the sea
and my daughter, pregnant
she's so far away from me now.

Sometimes, the freeway
that stretches out in front of me
is all I have, a soothing umbilical cord
between she and I, dividing my new life and old.

It's another over-the-rainbow weekend in the desert.
Search hard, and there's a new baby on the horizon
lighting my safe passage to shore in this desert,
this desert is an ocean of longing for love.

Tank Man

Me n' Andy drinking
Pabst Blue Ribbon
at Billiard's Bar
Highway 62, 29 Palms
Stater Bros. strip mall
(my boyfriend eight weeks dead,
suicide, shotgun to the head).

Andy hates the Mojave Desert
for no reason apparent to me
other than that he misses
forests and rivers and green things.

He says he can't wait to get home
he's done his four years,
three tours of duty in Iraq,
Afghanistan, he's just 22 years old.

He says
        Joshua Trees
        Grow between heaven's gates
        And the gates of hell. I read it
        In the Bible, in the Book of Matthew
        They're not even fucking trees
        And before I leave, I'm gonna
        Take my AK47 and blast one apart
        Just so I can say I did.

I'm on my first beer, he's on his ninth.

Joshua Trees, he says,
have bad vibes, they're a dark omen.
He sees Jihad flagellating, planting
IED's when the sun goes down
he walks through opium fields
he hears the call to fight.

Don't you get it?
It's fire season on the Mojave,
nothing to burn
but everything.

Thirteen Tuesdays of St. Anthony

Pray to the saint every Tuesday for thirteen weeks
perform the thirteen attributes of mercy

thirteen decades of three beads each,
the number of circles that make up Metatron's Cube

the days into the new year that some girls desert cities
and sleep in the open near sand dunes, like you

the total of one prophet and twelve disciples
thirteen turns makes a hangman's noose

Triskaidekaphobia, the fear of the number thirteen

thirteen eagles on the trail to the geoglyphs
the age a girl can join a witch's coven

the number of hours it takes to circumambulate
Eagle Mountain, in July, if you start at dawn

a great day of the month to see the face of God
Catholic or not, afraid, or full of new moon

the Virgin Mary I once loved
is still painted blue.

U-Haul Villanelle

I pack another box and look ahead
I sold the house, and now it's time to move
pictures of my life, the broken bed

dust so thick that I can barely breathe
these stories aren't so easy to remove
I pack another box and look ahead

my daughter's gone, the lovers off like thieves
the house and I know what we've all been through
pictures of my life, the broken bed

so little left, so much that I must grieve
I'm filled with loss, emptied by what grew
I pack another box and look ahead

I thought I'd sell the house and get ahead
I'm free, and full of you, I cannot lose
pictures of my life, the broken bed

I gather tools and then unbolt the bed
they've all erased me and so I must move
I pack another box and look ahead

pictures of my life, the broken bed.

The Ying Yang and the Cross

I left the suicide survivor's support group
early, because I felt like punching someone
or screaming at the top of my lungs, or worse
maybe laughing hysterically as others cried.

So I went on a hike in the Cahuilla Hills
pulled uphill by the power of the leash
past broken homesteader's broken stairs
past the grizzled miner's burnt cabin
the downhill hikers are afraid of me
the look on my face and my glares
but mostly they're afraid of my big dogs,

pulled uphill by the power of sundown
along a jagged trail slippery with loose rocks
along vistas that tower over the water tank,
we're the last ones going to the cross
the shadows have gotten deep and long,

pulled deeper into the wilderness
into our own reverie, the leashes disappear
the light bulbs on the cross suddenly appear
darker all around us, brighter up ahead
I turn to look behind and see them: three
teenaged boys, trying to catch up. They try.

We move faster, the dogs and I.
The cross pulls us along with a silent language
comforting in its hilltop perch visible from the
desert valley below, haunting in its persistent
stare, even the boys have grown silent until
they join us at the top, where I'm dumping
rocks from my shoes. No socks. I didn't plan

to come up here, I was glued to the dogs
who wanted to find something alive, smell
the scent of something dead, leave their own
small urine marks wherever they could, their
small nod to the coyotes lurking on the horizon
far above, crying their evening songs. I turn
to the boys, who have nothing to say, until I ask,

Why are you here? Planning to spend the night?
They laugh. The dogs sit still and listen.
I should offer a prayer, but I do not.
We're not here to hang out at the cross.
We're going to party at the yin-yang. Bye!
They pass me by, and I begin my dark descent.
I find it by iPhone. On Google satellite.
It's really there. The yin-yang, painted on a slab of rock.

Tortoise Heaven

Start from the tight-knit center
from a seed excreted by a condor
and nurtured by a drop of water

off the back of a saber-toothed
tiger, and suckle the melting ice
from the thaw of the Ice Age
when it tunnels, where it flows

one day they'll measure the
aridity of where you've been, the
depth and range of soils you've
known for 14,000 years and more

the underground love you've shared
with miles of other tortoise shells

It's then that you'll feel, and know
that your name will be King Clone

ruling your magic miles of creosote
filling the deserts in frozen eternities.

> *The King Clone creosote circle in the Mojave Desert is the oldest living plant on earth*

What Rises
2015

You, in your stripped-down kitchen
essential tools in knowing hands
hammer, circular saw, tape measure
the mouthful of blunt-tipped nails.

Me, hair blowing in the open air
convertible top rolled down this
desert night, swollen orange moon
embellishing my rounded thighs

while you re-model and plan
shift the room around you and put
the refrigerator against the other
wall, I change gears in a different

time zone in the desert west. I braid
my hair, untangle the ropy knots
of mangled string, while you cut
and glue and keep the wild puppy

from strangling on its chew toys
and you have the patience to deal
with this: unruly pets, disorder
in the kitchen, a woman roaming

deserts and mountains on loan
hammering the center of sunrise
into broken hearts. You work, I climb
another harsh peak and sleep late

nailed to bed in fading moonlight
I awaken, hungry, and your kitchen
still soon be in place, dog in cage
sun smoothing the beveled night.

Ruth Nolan is an author based in California's Mojave and Coachella Deserts. A former seasonal wildland firefighter for the US Forest Service and Bureau of Land Management throughout the Western U.S., she is now professor of English and Creative Writing at College of the Desert in Palm Springs, CA. Her fiction appears in *LA Fiction Anthology: Southland Stories by Southland Writers* (Red Hen Press, 2016), and she's most recently published poetry/prose in *The James Franco Review; Angels Flight Literary West; Desert Magazine/USA Today;* and her short story "Palimpsest" won an honorable mention in *Sequestrum Magazine's* 2016 Editor's Reprint awards. She's also published work in *Rattling Wall; Desert Oracle; Women's Studies Quarterly; New California Writing-Heyday Books; Lumen; Pacific Review; Rhino Baby; Poemeleon* and *The Desert Sun*. She writes feature articles about California desert culture and the environment for *KCET/Artbound Los Angeles; Inlandia Literary Journeys; News from Native California* and *Sierra Club Desert Report*. She's the editor of the critically-acclaimed anthology *No Place for a Puritan: the Literature of California's Deserts* (Heyday Books, 2009,) now in its second printing. She holds her M.F.A in Creative Writing and Writing for the Performing Arts from the University of California, Riverside-Palm Desert Low Residency M.F.A. program, and her M.A. in English from Northern Arizona University. *Ruby Mountain* is her debut poetry chapbook. She can be reached by email at ruthnolan13@gmail.com.

www.ingramcontent.com/pod-product-compliance
Lightning Source LLC
LaVergne TN
LVHW041551070426
835507LV00011B/1036